# SONNETS TO MY SKELETON

Roey Leonardi

*For my sisters*

# TABLE OF CONTENTS

## THE BOOK OF MARY

## THE BOOK OF EVE

## THE BOOK OF JAEL

## THE BOOK OF MIRIAM

# THE BOOK OF MARY

# Mama as the Ground From Which I Was Taken

Mama is what it means
to have a body.
She is smooth sun-spotted skin
beneath my baby cheek,
finger-twist curls that grow
like weeds when wet
down past her shoulders.
She is full-up and warm
in the bathtub with milky water
so deep it swallows her.
She is baby-I-can-see-your-bones.
I can feel her feeling them when
her arms are around me.
When I look at my reflection
I say, that is not me in there, that is the light
bouncing back a thousand colors,
that is a glass-shadow skeleton.
Mama doesn't like to not know me
beneath her hands. I can see her
on the end of my bed crying
because she doesn't know me.
*Sometimes it feels like I don't know you.*
Sometimes it feels like I never grew
inside her, *flesh of my flesh,*
*bone of my bones,* Mama
am I a piece of your rib cage?
If I saw the world as you do,
in gardens and infernos,
would loving me not make you cry?
My eyes have crossed themselves
since I turned six. They make two things
into one and one into two and heaven
and hell bleed together, but in the mirror
they are the only things that belong to me.
Too-large, blue then green then gold.
We don't know just where they came from.
I wish you could hold me in the empty
between your hips once more before

my body, which came from yours,
becomes unholy. I am afraid you won't love me
the same when I stumble cross-eyed
beneath your God, who I've found
in all the wrong corners of my skin.
He is in the knots of my knuckles,
spindly fingers too thin to fit your rings,
and you are singing
*oh be careful little hands,* but I can't
remember what to be careful of.
Mama I can't tell you all the things
I long for. When I forget how it was
to be a part of you, I rub my palms
against my closed eyelids and we
are in Eden, lying on our backs
looking up at that spiraling dark.

# Stand By Your Man

Through the window we can smell
last night's rain which we stumbled
through without noticing the chill,
soaked clothes clinging to ribs.
Out of it pours the honeyed voice
of Miss Tammy Wynette who we
are hearing for the first time,
but halfway through we sing
along as if we've always known
the words. And it feels like we've
always known the words,
and like we're singing them
from the same mouth,
from the mouth of one girl
who sits at a mirror propped up
by the window and lines her perfect
lips in pink. It feels like Miss Wynette,
who is dead in the ground,
is our Mother Mary, like her flesh
never withered away but is shining
beneath hair which is from-the-bottle
blonde. She's laid out like Venus
in the gauze of the bed canopy,
looking down on bare-backed
daughters, and I can feel my own
mother pull a slipping strap
onto my shoulder, and I can see
her at seventeen believing she's
in love while her parents fall out
of it, because love isn't perfect
and men are just men.
I sing the hymn of my sisters
and press powder on my nose.
Mama tells me I am worth everything
but the mirror tells me I am not enough.
Miss Tammy Wynette tells me something
is better than nothing and I am trying
to hear my own body,

my own mind which is just
another part of a body
I can only love if someone else does.
I look around at brushes
weaving through heads of hair
uncounted, golden in the sun,
at skinned knees, chipped nails.
I look at girls who are more
than two arms to cling to
and something warm to come to,
and Miss Tammy's voice is a gray ghost
whose bitter cold reminds me of my blood.

# For My Littlest Sister

I first spoke to you
through our mother's skin when you
were a whisper in her abdomen,
when you were a secret.
Before we knew if you would stick
like bugs in honey, songs
in head, words in throat. Little moth,
it doesn't hurt that Mama loves you
most, how could she not when
you look out the car window
and say *God is the yellow sun*
and it's that simple?
You made it true with your breath
filling places we never knew
were empty. In summer your legs
brown so old scratches glow
feather-white, and it startles me
to see you marked, to see
you touched. I'm sorry
we let the world touch you.
At night I check on you
and in the blue glow
you look drowned,
pressed flower, pinned monarch,
in stillness you are perfect.
Little nose, little veins on eyelids
crack like sidewalks into
your temples, into your hair,
yellow like mine used to be.
You are skipping sidewalk cracks
outside the grocery store,
saving our mother's spine.
I want to save you
as you are sweet shadow,
pin you to my heels
so everywhere we go,
I go first, to brush away
the spider webs tangled

between trees in the mossy
garden of our childhood.

## To My Mother at Seventeen

Your body is my body
only baby oil brown,
loved and unloved.
It does not trail behind you
like a shadow,
like cans tied to a rusted bumper
beating love songs
onto the pavement.
It holds you.
You lie out on the cement
till the sun turns your vision
cerulean and rippling.
You see the world
as I do. The heat
is a mother,
maybe Mary or Madonna,
and she grasps you
at the knuckles
and spins you round
and makes everything
dizzy and dew-dropped,
twelve beads of sweat
twinkling at your brow.
When dusk falls
with its firefly glow,
you fall back breathless,
wrap empty palms around
the cave of your ribs.
I am a promise
in your abdomen,
nameless as loose change,
and if you lost me now
you'd never know to ache.

# For My Sister Unknown

Who slipped from Mama's womb
like bird from nest.
Once, we found a nest of birds
left to starve and we nursed them
in the kitchen till they died
one by one, the pink
of their bodies too small to name.

If I could give you a name
it would be the sound
of catching breath after joy
shakes a rib cage and makes it ache.
I would give you the face
of the lady in the grocery store
bakery I watched frost cakes
as a girl. She'd smile at me
and make sugared roses
bloom from buttercream.

If you were here I'd make
a bowl of buttercream
we'd dye pink and eat
with silver spoons on the kitchen
tile till our tongues blushed
as though bitten.

Oh, how I wish you knew
Mama's hands, blackened
by the earth she spread
to keep you warm. I wish
you knew the sun.
That in August we would burn
the tips of our noses together.

I make you a grave
in my every footfall.
I've dropped pieces of you
like dust bunnies in the back seats

of friends' cars, beneath butterfly
bushes in grandmama's garden.

The empty you left
anoints the ground beneath me.
It is you, little sun,
that lets there be light,
makes us holy enough
to bury birds in a row
without losing our faith in flight.

Canvas Skin

Oh Venus,
born of the hands of Botticelli
and Cabanel, I wonder if they wept
when the shell pink of your lips bled
from their brushes. If the woman who laid
before Titian recognized herself remade
in the genius hands of man. Oh mother,
queen of lovers, skin polished
bright. Your body is the sun.
It is the reason my mother stores
stretch mark cream
beneath the bathroom sink.
She bleeds. Do you?
Four times a mother, her body
has been cut and torn, forty-six years
a woman it is freckled and lined, and yours
is white and smooth as baby
teeth in a little wooden box beneath
the pillow of my childhood bed.
Yours is the face of every fairy I've known.

Oh Olympia,
eyes stare straight ahead at your unseen
lover and at me as if we are the same.
Woman made sinner by Manet's hands,
was she cold as she posed, the paint
on her own fingers clinging,
illegitimate child. Oh whore,
teach me to wear my shame as you do,
like a flower tucked behind my ear.
Teach me to lay on my shower floor
and find strength in the parts of my body
not softened by rosy, heavenly light.
How dare you not hide behind a blue
veined wrist or the straight-laced mask
of motherhood, and yet, broad brushstroke
body, unflattered and unclothed,
you are warmer than sunlight and less pure.

Man like God created you,
mother and not wife,
rising from the sea to baptize
all sisters and daughters
in the unholy silver of your stare.

## Housefire

I have loved my body once,
at the age of thirteen,
the second month it washed
itself clean. I sat on my shower floor
and watched the water
between my legs blush rose.
It was beautiful
to have a body so alive.
Sometimes you forget
your body is alive
until you're bleeding.
My skin is fogged glass,
bruises forming fast like
noses and fingers pressed
against me, little windows
to look through and see the indigo
inside. Maybe the love I felt
was a love for a scarlet sun
on the once-blue horizon
of my hip bones. Red sky in morning,
sailor's warning. I was a siren,
blue, red, white lights in the darkness.
Now, there are times I think
that if our bodies are our homes
then we are trapped in burning houses,
breathing smoke the way
boys breathe "I love you"
to close the spaces between skin.
I want to love myself
in my bathroom mirror the way
I did at thirteen. Like each day
is that twenty eighth day,
and if I am a housefire
at least my mouth is full
of light, at least inhaled ash
reminds me of my lungs,
at least my fingertips glow crimson
with a heat given to daughters

by their mothers, a heat that does not
fade into blackened earth but goes on
and on, untamed and unspoken,
consuming the places we are bound to.

I first saw you in spring, overgrown with decay, kudzu, crabapple blossoms. My grandmother showed me the way, through a path in the woods near her home nestled in the red clay hills of upstate South Carolina. We drove to you in her little white golf cart while she called each tree by name: sourwood, crabapple, sassafras. She stopped to pick budding flowers and arrange them in sticky-sweet bouquets.

Her mind is an encyclopedia of all that surrounds you. You, the house where she grew up. I think it's a comfort to her, knowing the flora of the land you crouch on even as her memory of your interior fades. By law you belong to her brother. He lets you rot out of some age-old spite which no one seems capable of explaining to me. Your windows are boarded, your door is locked.

When I'm asked where my name comes from, I don't speak of its Hebrew origins. I speak of you, the crumbling artifact of a great grandmother unknown to me except in your terms. She and you tangle in my mind with stories passed down. She is in your kitchen sifting flour to make biscuits from scratch, measuring ingredients by an instinct that seems almost genetic. She pours coffee into a saucer with milk and cream so it will cool quick enough for my mother to gulp down before the school bus comes.

She is in your living room, too, playing the piano by ear. When the sky grows heavy and charcoal gray, she plays "Till the Storm Passes By," pleading for God to watch over her. On your front porch she teaches my mother to shell peas and snap green beans. She scolds her for picking all the camellias off the bush.

It makes me ache to think I will never stand within your walls, which are marked by a childhood of dirt roads and skinned knees that belongs to my blood, not my memory. I will not speak to the shadows in the corners, ghosts of the woman whose name I wear like a locket at my throat, the two short syllables, the misplaced letters: Roey. When strangers read my name they have trouble making sense of it, adding and subtracting consonants to create something more recognizable: Rosie, Rory, Roy. It is as foreign to them as the bamboo all around you is to the Blue Ridge mountains. My great grandfather planted it to shut out the wind, to lay you in a manger of quiet and still. It grew wild, flourished. I like to think that is how my great grandmother grew, too, within the white slats of her jungled oasis.

That first time you and I met, my grandmother told me the story of the dogwood tree outside your living room window. She pulled down a blossom and showed me the four powdery petals which make the shape of a crucifix. The splotches of rust like blood of the hands and feet, the green center pointed like a crown of thorns.

"God made it to remind us what we come from," she told me.

I come from you, I think, as much as I come from the city where I was born. As much as I come from my freckle-nosed sisters and my mother's backbone and the blue house where I first learned to ride a bike. We hold our origins before us like mirrors, to know ourselves through what we've left behind. You are my mirror, my closed eyelid. All that I see of you is what swirls in the dark. There is a proud woman who gave me only her name, resurrected. There is my mother and her mother each at seventeen, like me. We are as green as the Eden that swallows your caving bones in the impossibility of life.

# THE BOOK OF EVE

Sixteen

Some Friday nights I lie in bed and pray
to the shadow on the wall that my teeth will grow

wings and fly from my mouth, line up like pearls
on the throat of God and I will be a child again.

Pray my bones will stop sharpening
themselves like pencils, that when I shake

my head my thoughts will empty through my ears
the way my mother once promised they would.

That the spiders high in the far corners
of my room will crawl in the space behind

my eyes and weave their webs, drink from my tear ducts like oasis
pools in the brittle dry of my skull.

I lift my hands up into the mouth of the dark
which swallows everything too quick to taste.

Up to skinned knees, honey dreams, arachnid
angels, to all the things beyond my reach.

## Song From Skull

Your fingernails left etchings
in the music box shell of my skull,
changed the echo of firing neurons
into a song I don't know the words to.
I don't know the words to you.

You are the dark above mosquito-bitten
legs on the first night of summer,
moon-cast shadows beneath shoulder
blades hard and white as quartz dug up
from the yard and polished like baby teeth.

You are the empty of my parted
lips and at the back of my throat,
between legs, fingers, knots of hair.
Here are the places I picture you:

In your silver-windowed car
with rain beaded in your eyebrows.
Beneath Spanish moss with mud
on your cheek. Waist-deep in a river
that clings to you like children to ankles.

The folds of my sheets held up
like a tent make the contours
of your face. I let them fall, settle cool
onto each part of my skin.

You are the grout between shower tiles,
the thing I think of when I'm already sad
to make sadness a lover, so steady
in the blue beneath my eyes
I never want to be free of it.

# On Love and the Light Beneath the Door

When my father tells
my mother he loves her,
he says it like
*I'm sorry,*
like she's sitting
on the other side
of a locked door.
They're sitting with their backs
to one another,
rib on rib, spine on spine,
the wood between aching with breath.
Last weekend I kissed a boy
lying on a playground
beneath a bridge
with cars whirring overhead
full of empty cups, receipts,
lucky pennies, bodies pressing into bodies
in the shift from lane to lane.
All around me was black river.
I was silver.
My mother says love is a decision.
That at first it's a part of you,
like eyelashes, like fingernails,
but one day you wake up
and you choose to stay.
You have to keep choosing again
and again.
I am afraid to tell her
I can't decide what color
my own eyes are.
That the lashes ringing them
like spider legs do not
belong to me.
I don't tell her that sometimes
I look in the mirror
and I'm floating above my body
like a feather caught in wind,
suspended between concrete

and blackwater
in a layer of the atmosphere
reserved for last breaths.
The air there
tastes like honeysuckle
and asks for nothing.
When I shiver in the heat,
it wraps its arms around me
and I am enough and it
is enough and kisses
go nameless
like strangers driving home
to ground themselves
in their own bones,
to sing lullabies to the light
beneath the door,
to wake up neck stiff, deciding.

# Poem the Color of a Colorless Sky

Lately I wake up shivering
with teeth that chatter
like they did at age six,
blue-lipped in the public pool.
I forget I'm still young.

Tonight young is a stomach
that won't feel hunger.
It is falling asleep with only
my heartbeat. My body wants
to burn like wet gloves in snow.

In the cold, I am foreign
to myself. My mind sings
to my hands in a language
I don't speak. It buzzes
around my ears like God.

The Cannibalization of Adam

By Eve who sits at the stump,
serpent writhing river thin
at her waist. Sweeter than fruit
is the meat of the ribcage,
oil on lips like waxed apples

in the supermarket
where I feel eyes like pins in my skin,
cross matchstick arms
over my chest, poised to strike.

Once, my father and I trailed a deer
bleeding through God's garden,
my skin thistled and thorned
by the clinging underbrush.

Haunting hands cling to bodies,
ghosts of the first Virgin birth:
woman risen from bone
like a drumstick thrown out
on the beach for the gulls to pick clean.

In the leering eye
of the checkout aisle she
stands within me, counts
deadly sins on flower petals:

wrath, pride, gluttony. Each
rib we devour hardens our
skeletons like beetle wings,
shields us from stares down our spine.

The velvet doe does not desire
nor does she cry in pain.
She dies in quiet dignity, her hide
a cloak which blankets naked shame.

# Jellyfish Sting

This was when the earth
still carved my body alone.
Before I stole myself back
to be gutted by my own two hands.
The world found my form
in a block of rose quartz
and chipped it away with blades
shaped like sidewalk cracks,
green splinters, Mama's hands,
tentacles in the sea.
My first sting felt like a head
of hair, that same tangling.
Somewhere in the green murk,
that head was dipped in kerosene
and set aglow. I should have seen
it flickering. My father carried me
up onto shore and sat me down
and together we watched my salted
skin rise like braille and blush
beneath a sun heavenly white.
Before then, I thought
my father's arms were impenetrable
as the hands of God.
I watched my skin turn to a map
of a world whose seas I'd never
tasted and learned how
a body is meant to be marked.

Relearning My Bones

I do not know what color
to call my hair.
I would say it's like honey—
brown all together
and gold when spread thin,
but I don't for fear
I'm unworthy of a sugar
spun with wings.
I fall asleep
smelling like smoke,
like bees drowning
in motes of ash.
In the dark I have
no color at all.
I forget my eyes,
those paper lanterns strung
around my skull.
They are blue but I try
to fish green out of them
like pennies from fountains.
I want to taste something
sweeter than my own skin.
I envy the six-legged
who see in ultraviolet, who know
themselves in shades
I am forever blind to.

# Cutting My Ankle While Shaving

Skin pulled from razor,
the sea-glass translucence
of hollow cells while all around
the white of the bathroom bloomed
like poppies in Oz luring me
scarlet into a sleep that swooned
from my knees. I bled through
three layers of bandage and gauze.

When I was small I'd drip
sand on my legs and scrape
it away with a shell blade,
make-believe I traded for the ritual
of womanhood at age ten.
I lathered and went slow
and rubbed my shins together after
like a cricket humming in my bed.

There's a painting of Saint Mary
of Egypt when the monk Zosimas
found her in the desert. Her clothes
have withered away like moth
wings and hair flows gold from
her neck down, swallowing
the naked sin of her youth.

Maybe it's true and heaven
is somewhere over the Jordan
in a land of dust and hollows.
They say when they found her
she looked hardly human.
And so they immortalize her in oil:
woman with body covered in hair.

If I were to give up the world
it would start with the scars
on my ankles. I'd find
glorious rest not in the drowsy haze

of a thousand red blossoms
but in the comfort of my own bones.

Until then I hop towel-wrapped
to my mother's first aid kit.
The house spins around me into
the rolling russet of the Great Rift Valley
and I sink down skinned,
more animal than holy.

## Standing Before *Day (Truth)*, Ferdinand Hodler

In the knuckle-white walls
of a museum in Chicago,
I behold oil on canvas and say,
*She speaks to me,*
half-smiling. My mother sucks air
through her teeth,
says, unblinking,
*She has an eating disorder.*
I shake as I gulp air
that's known a thousand other lungs
before mine, oxygenated the minds
of those searching
for the things they cannot name
in blues and pinks and blinding light.
I try to find meaning
in morning embodied
in a ninety pound nymph.
She rises from a sea
like the backs of wisteria petals,
which I once scratched with my thumb
to smell earth's sweet breath
when I was still a stranger
to my bones.
As promised, she reminds me
of truth. Truth is a ribcage,
the knots of a spine.
It is lying to my mother
in a doctor's office.
It is undressing before the mirror
and holding my arms out,
wrists bent as though the sky
rests on my palms.
I want to hold the sky,
but I fear my mother thinks
I'm not that strong.
She says I'm too frail
for winter in the city.
She wants to keep me

in the day, in the sun
of her tangling arms.
Mama, if the painted lady
with her willow limbs
and tangling hair can birth
each day from her wiry womb,
I can leave you. I can leave
my mind when it leaves my body
to wither like gold marsh.
I will find a mother
in the shadow
who will braid my hair
and feed me truth till I am whole.
Don't you see how she stands
rooted as the oak
beneath which you sang
me lullabies? Don't you see
how she knows her place,
her sinew and skin
unyielding, aglow?

# Ode to My Hair

Or rather the pieces
fallen to the kitchen floor
which I can no longer claim
because they are not
attached to me.
And I have written poems
about losing hair,
but this is a poem for hair
I chose to cut off.
I had my father do it
in the kitchen
with sewing scissors
because it was thinning
out, because my mother
said it was thinning out
because of how little I eat,
because I feel like
I've swallowed the world
and I'm carrying it
in my stomach, and the world
is heavy, and I am heavy,
and each golden strand
is knotted to an anchor.
I can hear them clatter
like jacks while
silver blades sing
through the strands
with sharp snaps,
hungry jaws.
I have started to feel
hunger again. My body's
mouth sings to itself
even while I sleep.
It wakes me at night,
and my room in darkness
is a closed eye still sleeping
all around me, and in it
I dream I walk outside

and January pricks
my uncovered shoulders
with goosebumps, each one
a reminder of where,
in another life,
I sprouted feathers from my skin
and let the wind carry my body
high above the Earth
which knew me first
in its red clay womb.

# On Why I Write Poems About Bones

When I was six or seven, my mother found the skeleton of a bird in our side yard, distinguished from the front or backyard by seas of clover grown wild and herbicide free and sprigs of mint beneath the fence, which we'd pluck up and crush against the roof of our mouths with our tongues. I'd like to remember it bleach-white as poured plaster, but the bones were dingy, the beak and head half rotted. Feathers still clung to them like fingernails.

Looking back I am startled by how the structure of the bird was not so unlike my own, the frame of its wings morphed into hands over thousands of years of evolution, which is to say thousands of years of dying and decomposing into black earth.

I've decided when I die, I want to be burned and burned quick. Once my flesh is gone make sure they grind my bones down to a powder, and I mean flour-fine, no clumps of ulna or femur. I want nothing left that sinew could cling to. Let the parts of me I loved most never sit naked and dirt-streaked beneath the eyes of the living. Let them be free at last of the body they held upright.

I cannot pinpoint exactly when I became aware of the existence of my own body. But I can say with certainty it has haunted me ever since. Maybe it was at six, when I'd lie awake with my ear pressed to my pillow and listen to the echo of my heart. The beating turned to a thousand marching feet moving through my ear canal into my brain, and I let myself freeze over with the promise of my life droning on and on before me.

Some nights when I couldn't sleep, I'd crawl in bed with my older sister Grace. We shared a room then, two iron twin beds painted white with a nightstand in between. She'd usually push me out, but after we'd stay up making shadow puppets on the walls, birds that would swoop down to devour wriggling worms. This was before I knew I had thin fingers. I never thought I'd be so proud of my fingers, of the reedy bones that stand up on the backs of my hands when I wave them.

A few weeks ago, I asked my aunt to rub sunscreen into my back before going to the beach. As she did so in the cold empty of her foyer, she said, well-meaning I'm sure, "You're too bony, Roey." And then quickly on to how pretty my swimsuit was, how she'd loved seeing pictures from our family trip to the Keys, sweeping with hurried murmurs her earlier statement under the rug, but it clung to me, echoed later as I sat numb on the bathroom floor and thought that my own body was an impossible place to be.

I thought back to lying on the floor of my shower in sixth grade holding up a mirror, studying the curve of my waist like something that did not belong to me. Thinking the best parts of myself were the hollows between my ribs and my wrists which I could encircle with my pinkie and thumb. I was eleven.

In autumn of last year, I dropped fifteen pounds within a couple months. In December my father hugged me goodnight and said, "You're skin and bones." For New Years we stayed in a cabin in the mountains, and on a hike my mother looked at me and said, "Don't let her fall. She'll snap right in half." She told me I'd better stop getting smaller. I feel like I have to make it clear that I've never been overweight or underweight; I was only smaller. But I hid from her still, the calories I tallied up on my fingers and my quiet creeping to the scale in her closet each day.

At a doctor's appointment in January my mother brought up my weight. My doctor pulled up a curve of average BMIs for girls my age, girls whose thousands of names I do not and will never know, or whether they, too, are strangers in their own bodies. My own statistics were plotted against theirs. I saw weeks spent eating a handful of almonds for lunch and shaking in math class from drinking coffee on an empty stomach reduced to a single data point which had fallen from the rest like loose change.

"She's at a point where I would normally suggest sending her to see someone," my doctor told my mother. "If she can stop losing weight on her own, she'll be fine. But that's a chance I hesitate to take."

I protested. I thought of the money my parents would have to spend. I thought of the shame of admitting I could recite calorie counts like poetry. I thought, too much, of the horror of being forced to put on five pounds. In the end, I was trusted to care for myself. Afterward, sitting on the crinkling paper of the examination table with my hands beneath my legs, I said "I'm sorry" to my mother in a breaking voice. I'm not sure what for.

I don't remember when in my upbringing I began to equate beauty with being small, whether it was before or after I stumbled upon the decaying frame of a body the entirety of which could fit in my palm. I always liked learning about outer space when I was younger, the lesson where they'd tell you how many Earths could fit inside the Sun and how many Suns inside Betelgeuse and so forth until you could feel the solar systems lining your lungs imploding, because you were nothing, you were weightless. Once in the school gym they inflated this huge dome-shaped tent that was pitch black inside besides the projected constellations, and we all sat around with moons on our eyelids and there was no part of my body I could see. I was floating.

I can control how many calories I eat in a day, manipulate them till I see enough of my bones that I feel pretty, I feel whole, enough of my muscle and skin and fat that I feel human, that my mother's eyes do not look glassy at me across exam rooms.When I can't control things, I lie on my bed, back-flat to avoid my echoing heart. I don't rest my hands on my stomach because there, too, they are haunted by the soft, fleshy throb of my pulse. I wrap them around my ribs so I cave in on myself. I would rather hear the world breathing around me than the music of my own body. My bones are hard and hollow, constant beneath my hands, the only part of myself I have never failed to love.

All my poems are skeletal in one way or another. I think it's because I've found a way to make the ugliest part of myself sound beautiful. It is not beautiful to be in love with your own rib cage but it sounds that way when the hollows between are filled with shadow and breath and earth. I say I've found comfort in being small, in being not

Jonah in the belly of the whale but a hair on Jonah's head, or an eyelash drifting along with the seawater and krill, wish-wasted and water-logged. The truth is I can't find comfort in my own mirror. Maybe it was vain to look there to begin with.

So instead I fill all the empty parts of myself with pretty words. Honey pools in my clavicle; my hair drips silver down my spine; I hollow out my humerus with my father's hunting knife so I am light enough to fly to the forgotten nest of the side yard bird. Perhaps there are hatchlings there now with shadow puppet wings. I write sonnets to my skeleton until my fingers wear down to white, adorn myself in my own hatred, vanity, weakness, like garland wrapped around thinning limbs.

# THE BOOK OF JAEL

# Standing Before a Slain Bull Elk

Like David before Goliath
in a valley of Joshua and juniper.
As if God placed bullets
like stones in little pink hands.
Rain and sweat dripped

from my hair, christened
the Earth like holy water
while the soil reddened
with nose blood, tongue blood,
blood of the eyes and the ribs.

We tracked you over hills, rising gold
sea dragons. Along the way
I saw black fur caterpillars fall from trees
like acorns and writhe in the underbrush,
slept on the forest floor with sun freckling my nose.

My father and I laid awake in the cool
dark to hear your banshee call.
In death you were studded
with ticks like rubies, like pearls,
like your life was one of carrying

and of crawling. Once I met you
face to face my hands shook
with aching, with apology. Sometimes
I forget Goliath was not a giant
but a very tall man.

## Roadside Elegy

My father told me once
he was driving and saw bodies
flung out on the road, black
on the pavement like ants
dried out in summer,
like ants crushed
underfoot with still-wriggling
legs that move just to haunt you.
He stayed with a dying boy
till he slipped into unending sleep.

Once, I thought my little sister
was choking, and I crouched
on the ground and covered my ears
like it was not happening
if I couldn't hear it.
My father is losing
his hearing, and sometimes
when I repeat myself angry
he apologizes for
his body's own betrayal.

Sometimes I turn
from his voice like it it's not holy,
like it wasn't the last sound
on Earth heard by a stranger
in the grassy grave
of the median. I wonder what he said
and if the boy took it with him
inked across his eyelids.
I want to say to him: I'm sorry,
I'm sorry I'm not yours

the way I was when my hair
was new yellow,
and I'm sorry I made you stand
by the kitchen trash and tell me
no one loves you,

and I'm sorry I'm a person
who would crouch on the roadside
and block out the wails of sirens
like newborn daughters
when you'd sing them lullabies.

For Arden

I told you once
when I can't love my body
for its silhouette burned
on the backs of my eyes,
I love it for breathing.
When my mind bends the mirror
so my thighs become oceans,
I remember the bones inside them
that have carried me to every
single place I have known.

I know the way to your house
like I know my rib cage,
like we both know mothers'
eyes beholding rib cages
in summer. In summer
we'll gulp down
the sea and make
our mothers sleep easy
knowing our bodies are full.

My skeleton
carries flushed flesh up the stairs
to your room which is warm
and blue and holds us
in the creases of its palms.
We laugh till we ache,
till I can feel my body as whole
and not parts.

I want God
to be the feeling of laying on your
floor with cicada song coming in
through the window screen.
You were raised without God
while I was a shipwreck submerged
in holy water, but if He
is a happiness that fills you

up as it carves you out
then we are both devout.

When the ships of ourselves
are drowning in the garish brilliance
of a world too large
for the palm of a hand,
you help me stop fighting
for the surface.
Instead, we grow gills.

I forget that at one time each
person I love breathed through
gills in the indigo of mother
and womb. We crawl back
to ourselves as we were
before we knew everything,
to the dark place where
we must have met before,
as cells or as souls or as little
drops of water old as Earth.

Preparing Baitfish

My father sets two buckets
before me. One is full
of little gleaming fish
whose name I have forgotten.
It is easier to disembowel
something which has no name,
splayed with innards
laid out like glass beads.

The second sits waiting
for severed silver, abdomens
hollowed so as not to spoil in the heat.
*Start with the beak,*
he says, the needle nose,
clipped with pliers and tumbling
down into the empty
like porcupine quills, like blackberry
bramble nails ready
to drive through hand and foot,
empty places to fill when I doubt.

*Next pinch your fingers along the belly,*
releasing the sediment
of an ocean unremembered.
*Last are the eyes,*
stacked like checkers.
I drive a screw through both at once,
through the gray membrane between
where little fish thoughts
floated murky.

Around me the colors
of summer melt into one another
like cotton candy,
burning-sticky-sweet,
while my father hums a song
we once danced to
when I was small enough

to stand on the toes of his shoes.

Tomorrow he will take these
fish we have emptied
in their multitudes
and make them dance
like puppets through the sea.
His catch will last us
through August, stretched lazy
as childhood at our fingertips, both
our skin scented with the briny breath
of the water from which we came.

# For My Mother, Who Wishes I'd Write Happy Poems About Her

You see good like the way you peel
peaches over the kitchen sink
in summer, thumb-pressed blade
curling back the skin from the sweet.
I have yet to learn to make clean cuts.
When they cut me from your body
did you sing me the leather-bound
hymns of your childhood?
If there is one thing you have taught
me it is holiness. Once I dreamt
a man built from bone
plucked your heart from your chest
and handed it to me shimmering
and sucker-red. The brittle hard
of him dove into the soft cavity
of the body that created me
like blade into peachskin,
like a dolphin jetting up out
of the sea. In one of your dreams
God is a dolphin, in another
a man who walks beside you.
Mama here is a dream
I'll spin for you tonight
like black widow web.
Dream of God as a conch shell
pressed against my ear. Make him
echo in my mind when I'm alone.
Dream of Him as a thumbprint in indigo
ink that bleeds into the too-blue
river that cuts across my too-white wrist.
Dream you are God and I am the world
built up from your hands.
Let it be the seventh day
when we rest lazy together.
Look down with your great hazel
eye and see the nectar-sweet
good of the things you have made.

## All Hands Are Holy

At the end of my bed
baby sister twirls,
tells me of a crayon picture
she drew of God
*with high heels and shorts on,*
*part monster, part human,*
*part girl, part boy, it was so fun,*
she says, and I don't understand
the phrase God-fearing,
why fear what you could love,
what you could dance with?
My mother grew up skinning peaches
with pocket knives, humming from
the Baptist Hymnal, and she tells
me God doesn't care about
memorization, kingdoms come
or wills done. *Talk to Him like He's*
*your friend,* she tells me at age six,
feverish on my pillow.
*When you're scared know*
*He's holding you,*
*he's holding you in his hands.*
I've come to think all hands are holy
for everything they've known, touched,
held like sleeping children.
I see God in eyelids, freckles,
cobwebs lit up with sun,
exhale my prayers rambling
into my alarm clock glow.
He is the webbing between fingers,
rose-colored skin that reminds
me where I came from,
the water of womb, dark into light.

## On Fingers in My Hair

Which I wish was just-washed
and did not smell
like carpet and smoke
and mosquito bites.
I don't think you mind,
so I sink into white
like the heaven of my childhood,
like Jack plucking golden eggs
from the sky. I can give you
only gilt, which I lose in strands
like the ends of sentences.
It makes me ache,
the tangling and untangling.
I wonder if I'm cold to touch.
The baby hairs around my temple
curl into a halo light as spun sugar,
and I wish that's how I tasted.
I wish I could turn off my mind.
Sit in a dark that swirls with light
like the backs of my eyelids
and let the world wash over me.
I have dreams where
waves crash over my head,
a thousand salted baptisms.
Wake up stuck to my pillow
with frozen lungs until I peel
myself up like old skin
and gasp for breath.
I can feel you breathing.
You rattle like snake tails,
like a head-full of hissing
carving our bodies from stone.

# Because I Am Tired of Writing Poems About Bones

So here is a poem of flesh,
of clover caught in teeth
and the violent blue of summer.
In my too-small bed I dream of July,
a month in which I have yet
to know you. How its sun,
which is different from all other suns,
will color the curve of your cheek.

Let's go somewhere that makes us
feel small. Let's go to this beach I know
where you can swim out to a sandbar
that reflects the sky in a lattice
of shallow pools. Our eyelashes
will clump together like stars
and we'll lie on our backs till
the sun sets the world swinging,
hypnotic in violets and blues.

I'll ask you whether you think
your mother will sit on your bed
some September nights once you've gone
north, because I know mine will.
I'll ask if you remember the songs
she used to sing while you'd fall asleep.
How small we must have been
the last time we fell asleep like that.

I did not know you then,
and in September I may not know you
again, but I am not dreaming
of September. In my head it is July.
We are walking somewhere without shoes
and my hair is tangled with salt
and my skin is rough with salt
and I can feel my skin and on it
the heat of a home I still belong to.

## For My Sister Who Sings to the Sun

Lying side by side
on white gravel in Islamorada,
I listened to you pray
the sun would freckle your nose,
and you must have a voice
like peach nectar, that sweet,
to be attended to by a star.
But really I think it's more
like the skin, whose velvet
clings to tongue, demands
to be felt long after we swallow.
Your voice from the pit
of your lips demands to be heard.
If the clouds move aside
so your face can be flecked
with shadows of gold light
uncountable, it is only
out of reverence for
the unyielding stone of your
will. There are times I fear
I'll never know my own self
as you know yours.
By the light of the streetlamp
outside your window
we talk of the things
that have touched us,
and the pool of our shared
memory is miles deep,
but when I leave you
I know I will swim in its shallows.
Because it is you
who I've known all through
a childhood dappled dark
and light like the skin
of your cheeks, like the floor
of a forest. I have known you
thorn-scratched in forests
and salt-stung by the sea,

carried you shaking across
a mountain stream corpse-cold
and clear as the silver moon.
I have known many moons
and trees and streams
since the last time
I carried you. Now we sit
back to back and lean
against each other's spines,
the copper coils of your hair
winding around my wisps of gold.
I try to forget that soon
I will have to stand.

# Learning to Whistle On a Mountain in New Mexico

I leaned with my father
against Ponderosa pines
and drifted off, resting
on nothing but Earth,
a baptism in sun on leaves,
in caterpillars, in my own skin.
When we woke he taught me
to make the wind of the Gila
sing between my lips,
between the then-full
hollow of my cheeks.
Back home when he yells
I remind myself we are both
children walking in bones
that age around us.
He is seventeen.
He is fumbling through
a life struck like water from the rock.
My first memory is stinging salt,
his arms lifting me above
waves that crashed on sand
and stone. I did not cry
when he stumbled
because I knew
he would not let me go.
Back then he was as old
and as vast as a desert
and I was his drop of rain.
If we'd sat whistling on Mount Horeb
we'd be lambs led
from the Desert of Sin,
our path and place given
from God's hand. No more wandering
on legs carved from underneath us,
pulling music from shivering air
to drown words we flounder for
like fish drying out in a parted sea.

# The Joy of Taking

I have come to know my father best while trailing blood through the woods. Sometimes it is August and I am rosy with sweat. Others, it is December and I watch my breath leave my lips like the clouds of my childhood heaven. I breathe heaven over the body of a stiffening whitetail deer, my life reflected in its glassy eyes.

I must have followed my first blood trail before I could read. When the deer bled heavy and died fast, I'd help pick out the scarlet glowing beneath our flashlights, splotched onto yellow leaves and smudged against the bark of planted pines. When the trail was sparse, my father would leave me standing at the last drop so we didn't lose it. I'd stand alone in the darkness and watch the spider eyes winking up at me from the forest floor. Whenever he took me hunting, I spent much of my time waiting for him to return to me. I waited in tree stands, corn fields, forks in dirt roads, in the black and the cold, my little body humming with the promise that he'd always come back, and when he did, we would tell one another what we had seen.

I learned to recognize the pink froth of the lungs, the dark gristle of the gut. I learned to look for broken branches and trampled earth. I learned to let my heart beat quick when the trail grew thick, because around the next turn would be the still, silver body, the antlers jutting up like a crown of thorns. Sometimes along the way, I'd be caught in thorns and I'd cry out and my father would come untangle me, gently pulling briars from my skin and clothes with the same hands that would later drag the carcass through the woods by its hooves. After, I wore the scratches with pride, marks of the Earth which took from us as we took from it.

When I was thirteen, my father took me out west to hunt elk and mule deer in the Gila National Forest. We drove through Arizona and into New Mexico along an unending road which shimmered in pale green mirages where it met the horizon. All around us sprang up saguaros which faded into junipers and russet rocks like greedy fingers stretching to catch the stars.

I wish I could remember what we spoke of. I'd imagine I remarked on how strange it was that in the desert petrified wood was sold along the roadside like sweetgrass baskets back home, how back home I was learning in science class about the plates of the Earth that shifted beneath us. Maybe he told me a story about his own eighth grade class, reminded me of the child he used to be. I remember each time I looked out the window I longed for the car to stop. It wasn't an unhappy longing so much as it was restlessness. I wanted us to climb out and run, feet pounding, into that vast empty where we'd find something to hold on to.

When we arrived at the hunting camp, we stayed in a little cabin which was choked by the blue haze of pines. At night we could hear rats in the ceiling and the bugling of elk which is a sound that breaks over your head and crashes in your ears, wailing like a widow. I listened, entranced by a song I had never heard before and may never hear again. I know he was listening too, across the room in the dark. I laid warm and still and safe and we listened together to the crying of things untamed, untouched.


When I was small and yellow-haired, it was easy for my father to persuade me to accompany him. He'd lay out my clothes the night before, a bizarre assortment of camouflage and pink with two layers of fuzzy socks to protect my toes from the cold. He'd nudge me awake into a violet morning so early it was indistinguishable from night, and I'd get dressed and nod off against the window on the drive out to Green Pond or Eutawville or some other place swollen with green.

We always stopped at a gas station to buy coffee for him and hot chocolate for me, a bag of Cheetos and a bag of candy and sometimes an ice cream sandwich, which I ate year round with no regard for the cold. When we finally made it to where we were going, I'd stumble out of a car blooming with the artificial brilliance of junk food wrappers. I can remember him showing me how to close the truck door so it didn't make a sound, how to walk in the path he left so as not to snap twigs. He'd sweep branches back like curtains and hold them there so they didn't snap against my cheek. In the quiet I could hear everything inside and outside of me, the rustling of armadillos, the rattle of my breath.

He always had me climb up the rickety metal ladders of tree stands before him in case I fell. Once we were up there, shoulder to shoulder, it was a waiting game. We'd fill the spaces with I-spy and I'm-thinking-of-an-animal. When I grew restless I'd reach up to brush the hair from my forehead and he'd say, "Try not to do that. Your hands look like white flags to a deer." So I knotted my fingers in my lap.

He showed me how to look through the scope of a gun, my left eye squeezed shut to line up the cross heirs on a clump of grass in the distance. Through it, the world was a clear round picture like those windows you see on ships. I looked out into the blue, not knowing where we were going.

When we'd hunt in the evening, dusk would come and I'd be itching to go and he'd say, "Just a few more minutes. This is when they walk."

Here is something I've learned. When you're looking across a field of peanuts or a cutdown springing up with brambles, when you're looking at the pines on the other side growing up like teeth from the mouth of the earth, and you're searching for antlers silhouetted against the gray, for hooves and hide, your eyes conjure phantoms up from the ground. You see ghosts. You see the ghosts of whitetail deer that aren't really there. You see birds and bats flit and swoop. You see men floating through the underbrush.

I have never seen so many ghosts as I have in the hour of night when my father says the deer walk. I have never seen so many ghosts and been so unafraid.


I am reluctant to write about the times I have killed. I think it is because as I've grown older I've understood them less and less. I have stood before deer and before a great bull elk and buzzed with adrenaline and with my father's impossible joy. I have stood buzzing and felt I didn't have the right.

I do not fully understand the joy of taking. When I have taken it has been for my father who can hold the forest in his hands. He has earned it, I think, somehow, the right to uproot, to follow and to find. I do not understand taking but I understand him. I watch him skin and disembowel and I know I know, I know he loves the land that will one day swallow him, he loves the animal whose tick-studded body will fade into the roots of an oak whose acorns will feed the fawns in spring. He loves me.

I think the thing that startles me most about hunting with my father is the comfort I find in it. There is blood and there is dust and there are thorns in my hands and feet. But then there is gold sun kissing the treetops goodnight. There is a drift of wild piglets tumbling brown and cream and spotted over a fallen tree like little dogs. There is a mother bear and her cubs in the mountains of the Gila, *look through here, follow my hand, don't you see them?*

I know I will not hunt when I am old. And I will not know the earth as I once did, and when the birds sing it won't be for me. But wherever I am my father will return to me, lift me up from the crimson I guard between my feet. I will look into his face, into the joy that has filled the spaces between giving breath and taking it away, and I will thank him for all that I have seen.

# THE BOOK OF MIRIAM

## Would-Be First Love

My mother talks about you
like you belong to me.
Like you're tangled around my fingers:
Crabgrass, dental floss, hair
in the shower. A few nights ago
I pulled hair out of my shower drain
with a pair of pliers. It came up
from the gaping dark unending, like
weed from earth, snake from skin,
tooth from gum, like something alive.
I sat on the bathroom floor
and laughed at all the pieces of myself
I'd lost without knowing.
I lost you without knowing, and now
at arm's length you are as strange
to me as a hair from my own head,
uncounted and unnamed.
Earlier I thought of not knowing
you one day and the bruises
on my legs sang bluer.
I forget we were children together.
If at six I had risen from bed
to turn on the lamp and not hidden
from shadows beneath stifling sheets,
if I'd had courage in me then maybe now
my palms would not be empty.
My mother says don't let my hair
wash down the drain anymore.
I collect it on the edge of the tub
where it swirls into the eyes, nose, lips
of a face I might have known.

## Where I Slept Last Night

When I drifted to where
my body forgets to feel heavy
or hollow, I dreamt of your hands
grasping for mine- a kind of cold
like shaking on the bathroom floor
after sickness. And in waking, too,
my fingers were quill-thin and gnarled
like oak. Once, in my sleep,
our dream-selves were warm
and you pressed against my chest
in the place that now dips empty,
right in the center. I lie in bed at night
when I'm aching and feel the peach
pit shape of the bone between
my breasts. I think if I pressed down
my finger would break the skin
and plunge into my heart, bone-dagger
come back scarlet, all white things
come back stained. You keep me pure
beneath the crook of your shoulder
and we're both lighter than we once were
and I'm thinking of what we must
have carved out to get here.
Somewhere in the rosy gray of my mind
there is a dirt road along which
full cheeks and gap teeth decay
into the gold grass. The sun sets
and sparrows sing *In the Pines*
in my grandmother's voice. Where we went,
where we went, not even she knows.

For My Oldest Sister

I knew you best before I knew
my own body, before I knew shame,
before I ate of the tree
and discovered my serpentine bones.
You swallowed my empty
like gulping the sea.

When I dreamt of the green hand
stroking my back, I crawled in
beside you and we slept
with interlocking shoulder blades.
Sometimes I forget watching
sunrises over your cheek.

Forget bathing in the same tub
and make-believing with
the moonbeam on the carpet,
silver through gauzy bed canopies.
You'd cry when Mama went out
at night, dreaming her car would crash.

If I cried before you tomorrow,
you'd hold me like glass shards,
and I don't know if you lie awake
anymore, which dreams you remember
or the words that gargle in your throat
like saltwater in paper cups, like medicine.

Childhood was cherry-flavored,
cough drops to keep quiet in church.
Even now, when we bow our heads
it is you and I who keep our eyes open.
They meet and for a moment we are back
in twin beds sharing secrets,
the only two in the whole house awake.

For Hannah

When I was small and soft
and ate sugared berries
in summer, I wrote a letter
to God. *Dear God,* I said,
*I hope I get to die soon*
*so I can know you.*
I don't let myself remember why.
If heaven seemed that snow globe
sweet or Earth that hollow.

You tell me when you drive
through the night
you dream, eyes open,
of smashing your car
into the median.

Last weekend in our friends
bedroom, I held your head
in my hands like blown glass,
listened to the buzzing of bodies
down below and murmured
into the chasm of your shuddering
shoulders until the only words left
to my name were *one* and *two*
and *three*, our two breaths becoming one,
yours steadying while mine shook.

I wish I could keep the ghosts
of my fingers around your ears,
phantom flesh like a halo
blocking the shadow on your shoulder,
which tiptoes into your brain
like creeping down the hall
while the house is asleep.

You always rise in the still
before dawn. I say goodbye
to your silhouette,

fall asleep aching
for the hours in which
you are alive and I sleep
cheek stuck to the pillow.

I dream I steal the sun.
Weave it into a veil
to wear glowing around your bones,
make the dark places bright.
I want to keep you because
I can tell you which knots
in my spine I cannot love
and I can tell you I don't believe
in love and I can tell you

I still talk to God
without feeling like God
is the tooth fairy. You see Him
too in a darkness broken
by tail lights nightlights
glow-in-the-dark stars.

For Maclean

You taught me love is hands,
long rough fingers. Mine are cold
and at night I dream they are cut
from my wrists and withering into black
earth, emerald beetles beneath my bones.
We tell each other about our bones
and the bone-white scars
we've fallen in love with instead
of the bodies they mark, because
they remind us of all the places
we've been touched.
You draw faces on my bruises
in black ink and in the shower I pray
they don't fade, keep reminding me
that broken things are holy.
In the seventh grade school hallway
you baptized me with burdens I held proud
in the hollows of my collarbones.
I pooled secrets like copper chrism to anoint us
with the nectar of our childhood.
You like a prophet saw your life
stretched out and told me it wouldn't hold
the kind of love that lasts. Fingers too thin,
the milk and the honey stream down
between knuckles before we are full.
You haven't been full in a while, I can tell.
Lick your lips and let the sugar burn
your tongue, make it numb
to all other sweet things left untasted.

For Liv (Who Was Once My Mirror)

I scraped my knee once
and left rust colored raindrops
on your brother's bike.
The sky washed them away
months later, but till then
I was proud of the pieces
of myself we wheeled
through summer. We had yet
to learn how our blood cells hold
the holy text of our being
coiled around histones,
did not know to mourn
each microscopic death.
We did not know ourselves.
I knew you best when we
were green from nickel
stained rings, carving our names
in ivy for atmospheric eyes.
We could feel God then.
Could feel what it meant
to be young and have years
laid out like laundry with time to burn
our throats and lungs, denature
bodies we'd fall into
and out of love with.

For English

Little head with hair dripping syrup
slow over narrow shoulders,
I worry for you in the quiet
spaces. You are the beginning of summer,
of things we promise ourselves
that don't come true. You are sticky skin
bug-bitten in the violet dark,
which muffles our words with velvet,
with silk so that we can say anything.

You told me once that you brush
your teeth with the lights off,
and the thought of your brown body
hidden from its eyes in the mirror
makes me cold. Once, we laid
on our backs on your grandmother's
dock chirping and buzzing
with a happiness that aches,
one I swear I haven't felt since.

When I'm with you the world
swallows me; in the creek I float
under ghostly trees and forget
to feel heavy. Dripping
I drink Coke on the hot poolside
pavement and tell you about God,
my mother, my father, all the things
I cannot make myself enough for.
I think we find the same places holy.

Sometimes I wish I'd known
you when I was small, when the Earth
took its shape in the Genesis of my being.
I wish I could reach you
in that far off place you go
when your eyes are smudged
with graphite shadows, empty
as the bottles we find broken against trees.

I'm scared we'll never drink
our share of being this young.

Things I'll Leave Behind

I want to remember all the places
I laid down when I carried
too much in me to stand.
Lately I am laden more often than not.
I've felt my chest cracking
open at the bone. The husk of me
aches to fill itself up while it can.
I want to fill my body with bodies.

With boy who brushes ink
off my cheek and tells me
which lane when I drive to a place
I've never been. I could bite
my nails to make my hands
into his and remember
how they cupped
the curve of my cheek.

With one little sister in the front yard
spinning her brown body
like dandelion seed in wind,
the other wilting her skin
in the creek. When I leave
the shell of my room and crawl
unclothed to colder water
I will paint my nose with mud
and think of lying in clover
penny-bright and watching them
flit above on the oak tree swing.

With girls stretched out in a billowing
bedroom, windows open to the promise
of spring. I'll lacquer my lips
in red like we did in the still
between nights when we were too much
skin, or else too much bone.

With Mama in her big white bed,

the only person I know
who can build a God
in the air above her head
with the sound of her own breath.
I lost her ring in autumn,
too long ago for confession,
but I'll picture its opal, gold
in sun like the twists of her hair
which my father fell in love with
when he shed his skin and home.

I've found the shed skin
of snakes in the roots
of papery trees and I wonder
if the raspy shells of us will remain
once we leave the place
where we grew up,
mothers pressing us between
the pages of Bibles,
baby's breath to help remember
who we were before we were.

## Swimming in a River

That cuts through the Blue Ridge
silver like kitchen shears
and teems with flat-bellied
fish that mirror the sky.
Minnows part around bare feet
as if holy, as if the Red Sea
were made not of water
and salt but of scale and bone
and white flesh.
We are prophets
with freckled legs growing
like stalks of bamboo so fast
they tangle. We are bodies
that have fallen in and out
of love with one another
and with our own selves.
When our fingertips whiten
and wrinkle, we'll lay
reptilian on sun-hot rocks
and my unbrushed hair
will dry in ringlets like my mother's.
This is how we leave our mothers.
How we leave our brick homes
and the notes we penciled
onto closet walls. Our hiding
places will go empty now.
We are ducking our heads
under cold clear water
to see through fogged glass
the faces of those we have loved.
Dressing beneath the shade
of an oak we linger
in the Eden of our own purgatory,
eating the green of sourwood trees
like forbidden fruit.
Its taste tempts us to build
a home in the treetops
but deep down we know

our cradles have fallen.
So we stay just a while longer,
pick through our childhoods
like coyotes through carcasses.
The best bones we keep
and string into armor,
your clavicle over mine,
a shell I will someday shed.

When I think of Edisto I think of peach soda. It drips from the corners of my mouth and down my chin, fizzes sweet and warm in the pink spaces of my gums because that place has known me long enough to know my baby teeth. I keep the Nehi bottle caps in a box beneath my desk like smooth pieces of jade. It coats your insides in sugar and stains your tongue, so when you speak your words are creamsicle colored with artificial flavoring.

We buy them when we stop at King's Market, cooled by lazy electric fans in the dripping heat. There's violet onions and still-green bananas and chickens in a coop out back in front of the U-Pick, U-Buy strawberry fields. My mother always gets boiled peanuts and a key lime pie, and the sodas for us. We open them using the old Coca-Cola bottle opener mounted on the wall even though the caps are twist-off.

On the way to the easter egg beach houses we drive through the island. If Edisto were Eden then God must have looked down on it and said "Let there be green." We breathe it in and learn that the color green smells like salt and earth and wood fires burning. It's in the oaks bending over the road, the marshes swelling up with golden light, ivy running up the edges of little ramshackle white houses set back from the road. They twinkle with Christmas lights year round. When I see those lights I imagine them through a long dark night, inviting me in. They are baby-rest-your-tired-feet lights, I can tell, and it makes me sad to know I will never be called by them through the shadows.

Edisto is my childhood best friend. I see Delaney in the sunroom sitting on the swing bed. That room is full of light, too clean to be called golden, filtered by the dried out fronds of palmetto trees just outside the many windows. We are laughing until our bodies ache and soon my mother will pull me outside to scold me for being so loud but it won't matter because it is summer and we have the whole weekend here and look inside at that great white bed hung from ropes and all that cloud-mist light.

I have known Delaney nearly my whole life. Our parents were friends, and while all three of my sisters loved her I was the one born lucky enough to be her same age. We were each other's, in that way.

When we were little she was sharp-boned with the kind of hair chlorine could turn green and big hungry blue eyes. I remember her in a striped swimsuit in the outdoor shower beneath the house. The white vinyl curtains blew against us, sticking to limbs we had not yet fallen out of love with. We peered out from behind them to spy on the neighbors who had just come back from the beach with beer bottles and flip flops in hand.

"I think they saw me," Delaney would say and we'd shrink back still and quiet, holding our breath until we couldn't contain our laughter at one another's flushed, swollen cheeks.

At night we slept in a pale blue room with white bunk beds. My older sister Grace and I slept up top, while little Sophia and Delaney slept on the bottom. This was at times a topic of heated discussion, so some nights I'd take my turn down beneath, or else Sophie or Delaney would squeeze in with me up so high we bumped our heads on the ceiling if we sat up too fast. Grace and Delaney liked to hang upside down from the top bunks and let their hair swing down in the darkness. Sophia called the shadowy strands "black bats" and would laugh when one would descend abruptly from above. One night Grace hung herself upside down till she was sick to her stomach, and afterwards my mother and Delaney's alike banned "black bat" or else we'd all have to sleep in separate rooms. They still did it, of course, only quieter now.

When my youngest sister, Willa, was born, she was put in the porcelain colored room next door, forcing us to whisper at nights. We were ten then, and Delaney told us about boys named Josh and Benjamin and Skye whose names we turned into rhymes and songs. After she'd heard enough from us about sitting in trees and first comes love, then comes marriage, she'd cross her arms and roll over, saying "I'll never tell you a secret again."

We'd plead with the shorn wings of her shoulder blades till she thought of another story with which to tantalize us. Then, she'd prop herself up on her elbow and yawn, "Oh, alright then," and continue to gossip, her face lit up by the flashing lights of cars going down Jungle Road.

One night we turned the bunk beds into a fort, hanging blankets from all sides and forming a canopy over the space between them. We stayed up until the morning playing truth or dare and sucking on lollipops from the island candy store, falling asleep around six tangled in quilts and waking with the noon sun lighting up knotted hair before our eyes like the thin filaments of light bulbs.

The beach on Edisto has become increasingly crowded as I've grown older, dotted with cheap plastic buckets and umbrellas, but compared to the shorelines closer to home it is barren. Delaney and I used to pick out a house as far away as we could see and tell our mothers, "We're walking to that short orange one way out there, see you soon," and we were off. The shore is separated by man-made rock barriers and we liked to explore them on our way. The granite grows slick with green algae and glints in places with the sharp-edged lips of indigo barnacles. In the crevices there are deep wells where little anemones blossom scarlet and snap shut at the touch of a finger.

"That's what a kiss feels like," Delaney told me once, her face grave. I didn't believe her but I nodded anyway.

When we weren't walking we were swimming. We were never ones for lying around. Stormy days were the best ones because the waves were swollen and violent. You had to fight to keep anchored in one place and it made your legs tired but it was a good kind of tired. It was good to be held up by skin and bone in the midst of something so angry and so strong. When the sea was calm we'd lay on our backs and let the waves lap over our faces, pretend to wash our hair with sea foam. We'd feel with our toes for the sharp edges of sea shells and pull them up, skip them across the surface.

Once, Delaney's mother drove her and my sisters and me out to Edisto Island Presbyterian to visit the graveyard, which is supposed to be haunted by the ghost of a girl named Julia Legare, buried alive. Little Julia won't keep the door on her mausoleum now. She flings it open each time. We went inside it, cooled by dirty marble, standing before the wall behind which her body must still lie. Outside the sky was gray and gold and Spanish moss dripped silver among all of God's green. Delaney reached over and squeezed my hand. Ghosts only latched on to empty palms anyway, so we were safe to let ourselves feel fear in the closed eye of a grave, safe to snap ourselves awake through the ever-open door.

We drove home with the windows down even as it began to rain, covering everything up in little glass shards that caught the light coming through the clouds. "The devil's beating his wife," is what Delaney's mother used to say whenever the sun and rain streamed down together like that.

I have not seen Delaney in two years now. Our families grew apart and so did we, for reasons that were neither of our faults. Too much water for little legs to hold up against. I guess after all that it wasn't enough to keep being friends just because I can't remember a time before I knew her. I still talk to her now and then, but never in person. I wonder if her eyes are still large and starved for sight, if they take in everything with wonder and greed. If they'd take me in, after so much time, take me out of the dark to sit on a peeling front porch surrounded by colored lights like they'd known me all along.

About a week ago I went back out to Edisto. We were spreading new gravel over the driveway and once the work was done I walked to the beach, laid on a towel and let the wind blow against my eyelids till tears streamed down the sides of my nose. The sun was so warm and so bright and I was full of a kind of happiness I've come to know at seventeen. It's not pruned skin, aching bones happiness. It's peach soda. When I taste it I know the sweetness will not last. It scares me sometimes how I can lie with the earth pressed up against me, with the Devil's wife weeping her cool tears just beneath my rib cage, and be so violently in love with everything the way ten year olds are in love with boys' names that I know I will fall, I will crash.

It scares me that if I saw Delaney tomorrow it would take me a moment to recognize her. I thought of that while I laid there holding my own terrifying joy in the space between my collarbones. In that place, on that green island, I know her. Maybe not her now, but I know her as a six year old asleep on the couch with a sunburned nose. I am there beside her. Our fingerprints are smudged on the sunroom windows, baby hairs tangled in the dust bunnies beneath the bunks. We've rubbed lashes from salt-stung eyes and they remain buried in sand at the bottom of tidal pools. A part of me is there, digging them up, collecting them like my mother collects shark's teeth on the back of her freckled hand. We made wishes on them once but those died or came true long ago. Now they remind of us bodies small and new, happiness measured by the backs of our eyelids, lips stained with the nectar of summers so sweet we taste them long after we've forgotten our names.

# ACKNOWLEDGMENTS

I would like to thank my mentor, Emma Bolden, for your guidance. You have been more supportive and dedicated than I ever could have hoped, and I am so grateful.

Thank you to my mother for teaching me to have faith and to my father for showing me the value in hard work. Thank you to my sisters for sharing with me their secrets and fears and dreams. All my strength comes from you.

I would like to thank my teachers, F. Rutledge Hammes, Beth Webb Hart, Danielle DeTiberus, Sean Scapellato, and Rene Miles. You have helped me grow as a writer and a person and have challenged me to push myself, sometimes unwillingly, to be the best I can. Thank you for making a home for us all and reminding us not to throw eggs at it.

I am indebted to my creative writing peers for seven years of acceptance and comfort and incomparable joy. Adam, Liv, Chassee', Elle, Chloe, Maya, Reese, English, Trammell, Arden, and Braedon, each of you has humbled me with your talent and character. I feel so lucky to have known you and to have read your work, which is to have seen the world, all its shadow and light, through eleven pairs of eyes each different from my own.

Made in the USA
Las Vegas, NV
23 April 2021

21910780R00052